THIS NOTEBOOK BELONGS TO

CONTACT

EMDR   9th Mar

Eye **m**ovement **d**esensitisation and **R**eprocessing.

Accidentally developed by Francine Shapiro, 1987.

EMDR works with intergrating new experiences into an individual's existing network of memories.
Typically, memories are processed and asimilated by an individual through thoughts and beliefs, based around past experiences and understanding of themselves. This happens whilst we sleep. Memories are filed away, like ph in an alb

Frozen Memories
Sometimes an experience has such a traumatic impact that the memory is no processed in this way. It becomes 'Frozen unprocessed by Brain, and attached to the negative emotions and physical symptoms that accompanied it, when took place.

Brain Lateralization

Left	Right
Analytical	Intuitive thought
Thought	Nonverbal
Planning	Creative Art
Maths/Science	Imagination
Logic	

No definitive explanation on why EMDR works — process stimulates left and right hemisphere simultaneously, which is thought to mimic how memories merge and are processed during dreams or REM.

Exercise 1 - write why stimulating both areas together allows the memory to be integrated into normal memory system

- It mimics how memories merge and are processed in sleep
- It allows the individual to reexperience the memory, whilst safe in the present, without the negative emotions / physical symptoms

Exercise 2 - write 3 tasks left + right Brain control

Left - planning, analytical thought, maths

Right - Intuitive thought, imagination, Art.

Key learning points
- Left + Right brain
- Founded by accident
- Mimics memory processing in sleep
- Isn't fully accepted as a treatment, but has gained recommendation by NICE.

Part 1

Understanding EMDR means understanding the adaptive information processing (AIP) model that guides it. The model is based upon the idea that the brain processes new experiences into an already existing memory network.

E.g. A child's experience of sharing a toy may include the thought 'don't want to' as well as lessons such as "It's ok, we can share, it's still my toy". This is assimilated into memory networks related to relationships, as well as self determination and conflict resolution.

New, similar experiences are further integrated into these memory networks, thus allowing us to make sense of our new experience in the context of what we already know. This is called Adaptive Info Processing.

Each time we face new situations or experiences, we automatically link them to the relevant memory network, building further on our perception of what's going on in tandem w/ feelings + behaviour.

According to Shapiro, when we experience something particularly distressing, the memory is not processed the same way. The memory is stored in own, neutral network, unable to connect with other memory networks that hold adaptive information. Thus, the initial distress can continue to be triggered by different stimuli — thoughts, feelings, people, sound, smells.

The aim of EMDR is to 'unstick' the brain's hardwiring so that neutral pathways accessing trauma can be found, then moved into normal, adaptive memory networks.

Case study: (from 'Getting your past right' by Shapiro)

Man comes to therapy (EMDR) per sexual impotence.
He identified a memory, following parents divorce where mum said "You're doing a bad job of replacing Dad".
Then, mum fell ill, had to put her in a home. Feelings of guilt, how he'd disappointed her, not a real man. Thus, impotency. Physical expression of inadequacy.

w/ EMDR, was able to identify memory. See error of responsibility placed on self, remove feelings of ineffectiveness. Sexual abilities returned.

Lateral Stimulation is visual, auditory tactile stimuli occuring in a rythmic left/Right pattern.

Four main effects of Bilateral Stimulat[ion]
* a sense of relaxion, decreased arou[sal]
* Increased attentional flexibility
* A distancing effect (problems further a[way])
* Decreased worry.

BLS works in a similar way to how the brain usually processes info - physiological effect first (physical tension) lifted
Psychological effect (eg decrease wor[ry])

The Working Memory

operates over → temporary → Manipulate → Focu[s]
a few seconds   Storage   Info   Atte[ntion]

It is likely that BLS disrupts working mem[ory]
long term memory - vast storage capacit[y]
Working memory - does not
In EMDR, a disturbing memory is brough[t] into 'working memory', then BLS, we end[up] exhausting or disrupting working memory b[y] focusing on two things at once.

REM sleep:

(EMDR also engages similar brain mechanisms as those underpinning rapid eye movement (REM sleep).

During REM sleep, our eyes start to move rapidly from side to side, while breathing + heart rate speed up. REM sleep, mixed frequency brain wave activity becomes closer than that to an awake person.

During REM - we have our vividest dreams, due to heightened cerebal activity. While REM dreams feel hyper realistic, arm and leg muscles become temporarily paralysed, prevented from acting out the dream.

In this state, individuals can process events of the day, repiling and consolidating them into memories, eliminating information deemed unnecessary.

BLS is only one part of EMDR, and must be used with an internal state of physiological arousal for it to be effective. It is the dual focus of attention which unsticks the memory.

In EMDR, if you use BLS w/o traumatic memory, you'll fail to achieve anything. Equally, if you arouse internal distress without the addition of BLS, you may end up re-traumatising yourself.

AIP - the brain processes new ~~mem~~ experience into an already existing memory network.

When we experience something distressing, the memory of it becomes stuck and stored in own neutral memory network, unable to connect with other memory networks that hold adaptive information.

EMDR is based on the idea that negative thoughts, feelings and behaviours are the results of unprocessed memories, it doesn't require digging deep into these memories.
However, clients are asked to create a picture which relates to the trauma to hold in their mind. Then, they will use their own rem or rhythmic stimuli to divert attention from the image in their mind, thus dampening the usual emotional/physiological consequences.

Benefits of EMDR
- successful results with severe PTSD, addictions, chronic fatigue, migraines.
- doesn't have to be severe, hurtful childhood experiences, painful breakups, or general 'stuckness' can also help with.
- can benefit all ages (children + teens)
- may also help obesity

Many of us subconsciously hold self-limiting beliefs based on unhappy life experiences.
When this happens in childhood, we often subconsciously look for self-fulfil ways in our subsequent adult life to show us that these beliefs are true.

Physical benefits
Often when carrying around negative beliefs and feelings about ourselves, they manifest physically. Eg, someone who experienced neglect, and a sense they are unimportant may spend their life trying not to take up space.

The Three pronged Protocol

Shapiro established a specific protocol and framework to help guide therapists in overall treatment of a client. It consists of 8 Phases.

In EMDR, attention is directed to 3 time periods: past, present and future.

Past Events
- childhood, often the basis for negative beliefs
- Once the belief is formed, the conscious mind looks for evidence to support it.

Present
Once you have processed details of the past events that have set the groundwork for the disturbance, you can shift focus to processing specific triggers.

Higher Order Conditioning

Shapiro noted that some triggers remain active, even if original traumas have been processed. The reason behind this is that they have not, in fact, been fully processed or it is a result of 'Higher order conditioning' whereby another previously un-accessed memory network is now activated by the original cue.

The future template

The treatment is focused on helping the individual visualise successfully managing an anticipated future event.

There are 8 Phases

* history taking
* client preparation
* desensitisation
* Installation
* Body scan
* Closure + Reeval
* Assesment

History Taking.

In a proffessional setting, you would be asked to share your story, find out why you are seeking EMDR, etc.
The therapist will attempt to discover touchstone events; ie previous experiences that contribute to current symptoms.
As you review these events, you'll be asked to rate how disturbing they are, 1-10.

A target sequence plan is developed.
Review of what affects you from past, and also a template of future triggers.
At this juncture, it's important to identify coping techniques you can use in the moment.

Preparation ②

Identifying if fully ready.
Identifying how to self soothe
Introduce specific grounding exercises

Assessment ③
- Forming a picture of the target event
- Identify a negative cognition
- Identifying a positive cognition.

Picture — may involve person, place, or activity that best reflects the event

Negative cognition — the belief that you associate with the target event, rated on a scale of 1-7

Positive cognition — a belief which contradicts the above, and feels suitable

Rate how true it feels 1-7.

Desensitisation ④

° Focus on the targetted event using the image developed in assessment. Once you feel associated sensations, the Bilateral stimulation can start.

You will be instructed to move eyes back and forth, follow finger, light on screen or tapping on both sides of the body which is generally done when self administered.

You continue to focus on the target image + the eye movement simultaneously while remaining open to anything that comes up.
Stuck memories will start to shift.

Some therapists use interventions called cognitive interweaves.

Then, rating 1-10, disturbance. When rated at 0, the target truly feels neutral and not distressed you will move to Phase 5.

Installation ⑤
It is here that the positive cognition is introduced. You can use more than one. Scale it (1-7) until you achieve a 7. Bilateral stimulation continues throughout.

Body Scan ⑥

You will be asked to mentally scan your body to see if there are any residues of tension related to the target event, still remaining. If an return to BLS.

Closure ⑦

At the end, you should feel a sense of closure. You may need to employ self-soothing techniques.

Re-Evaluation ⑧

Check treatment is having positive impact.

History-Taking ①

to identify what kind of distressing or unpleasant experience they want to deal with

The general framework, is to ask clients some of the challenging symptoms, behaviours and associated beliefs.

e.g.
- Unexplained crying outbursts
- A sense of rejection
- Panic Attacks
- Fear of walking alone
- Anxiety during presentations

Therapist should ask about
- Past medical history - complications, trauma
- Medication History
- Family history
- Social history → drugs/alcohol, housing, pets, hobbies
- Systems - cardiovascular, respiratory, gastointestinal

* <u>Uncover Touchstone Events</u>

* <u>Identify negative beliefs</u>
(not good enough, I'm a loser, I'm not safe)

* <u>Future Triggers and coping mechanism</u>
- Where might the person be triggered
- What can they do to cope/sooth

~~Side Event~~

<u>Preparation</u> ②

Ensure client understands EMDR
Make aware of side effects
 - Fatigue, flashbacks, dizziness, lack of concentration, hyper-sensitivity, hypervigilance, difficulty sleeping

Share techniques !!!

Breathing exercise - Take 10 slow breaths. Focus attention on each breath, say/ number of breaths to self yourself as you exhale.

Mindfulness Exercise no. 1

Set an intention.
eg. "I want to feel safe".
Now sit with eyes closed and focus
on breath, inhale deeply and slowly,
before exhaling. Bring to awareness
the present moment, noting the
sensations of your body, skin, sounds
Focus on being present right here.

Mindfulness no. 2

Hold hot tea or cold water. Inhale
scent, small sips, feel comfort of
drinking the tea.

Meditation - Body Scan

Sitting or lying down, close eyes,
begin breathing deeply and evenly
Focus on sensations in body
Attention from Head to Toe.
Notice agitation or pressure
and breathe into those places
feel body expand w/ each breathe

Stretching

- Interlace fingers, raise arms above head, palms up
- Arms in line with ear
- Look straight ahead, shoulders relaxed
- Hold for 5 full breaths
- Let arms fall down to your side, roll your shoulders back and forth

Repeat.

Stretching. Heart opener — helps feel safe (Yoga po...)

- Stand with feet hip distance apart
- Reach hands behind you, clasp at base of back
- Look straight ahead, lift clasped hands as high as you can behind you. Pull shoulder blades together

- Inhale deeply through nose, exhale through mouth x5

Self Soothing Techniques

The Safe Space

As EMDR can bring up feelings of not being safe, it is vital that you can focus on a safe place during difficult moments.
Think of somewhere which makes use of all senses, use a photo or drawing if it helps.
Practice conjouring it, to transport with ease.

The Butterfly hug

Cross your arms and rest each hand on opposite shoulder
Focus on breathing
Think of safespace
Tap self on shoulder 6 times (when calmer)
Take a breath, and repeat.

Example of History Taking

Your Past - What memories/past events cause distress just to think abo[ut]

Your present - What are your current triggers / challenging issue[s]
— What negative beliefs

Your future - What future incidents may trigger you?
What are your goals? Can you see where your issues may be holding yo[u] back? What skills + qualities do y[ou] lack, and what " " would hel[p] you achieve the goals?

Assessment

Choosing a memory to target
Collect a list of 10, rate in order of disturbance
or 'group' memories that are most directly
linked with presenting symptoms, then
target a representative memory of the
grouping.

Kitchur's Genogram approach

```
  ☐      ○              ☐      ○
GrandF  GrandM         GrandF  GrandM
  |                       |
  ☐ ─────────────────────  ○
Father      |    |    |   Mother
            ☐    ○    ☁
           Bro  Sis  oneself
```

genogram was used by Maureen Kitchur
to map family relationships + key milestones, including trauma.

Forming a picture of a target Event

Select a memory, then form an image of it. A picture is anything that elicits an emotion and physiological response. Eg. face of peprator, a place or activity. Smells or sound

Therapist - ask a variety of Qs re event, what happened, when, where, who.

Identifying Negative Cognitions (NC) an Positive Cognitions (PC)

All experiences teach us something about ourselves or prompt us to assess ourselves in some way, and to form beliefs based upon o memories. According to Shapiro, the major of the ideas we have about ourselves are for during our childhood, and become self-fulfilling as we grow older. Negative sel beliefs can cause us to make poor choice steer us in directions that are unsafe or inappropriate, even if we're unaware. The are not truths but verbalisations of the disturbing emotions that still exist as a result of the negative experience.

In Getting Past your Past Shapiro identified 3 main categories of negative Cognition...

Responsibility - Feeling flawed or damaged in some way, such as not being good enough, being unlovable, ugly, stupid - feeling "you're to blame".

Safety/Vulnerability - Feeling in danger, that you're trapped or that you're going to die

Power/Control - Feeling powerless and unable to depend yourself in various situations, feeling you don't matter or that you're invisable

Positive cognitions (PC)

A positive cognition is a belief which contradicts the negative belief.
Ie 'I am unlovable' → 'I am lovable'.
'I am not safe' → 'It is over'.

The Subjective Units of disturbance (SUD)

10. Unbearable
9. Feeling desperate
8. Freaking at
7. On the edge of some bad things, can contro
6. Feeling bad – something needs to be done
5. Moderately upset, uncomfortable
4. Upsetting feelings that don't feel good but ma
3. Mildly upset
2. A little bit sad
1. No accute distress
0. Peace

The Validity of Cognition Scale (VOC)

1–10
completely false, completely true

How you feel, not how you think.
We may logically know something isn't true, but it might still _feel_ true

Installing positive thoughts

Tapping In

Emotional Freedom Technique involves tapping w/ fingertips on specific meridian points while talking through problems / negative feelings.

This is not the same as the 'tapping in' of EMDR.

    Thinking of a resource (image)
    Tapping right - left, right left
    for a short period, 6-12 sets

Using Safe Space
If emotions become overwhelming, go to your safe space, and use 'butterfly hug'.

When the target event has reached a low point on SUD Scale, and the individual is satisfied it has become neutral, it's time to replace the negative cognition w/ a positive one.

First, it must be marked on the VOC how much a person believes their chosen PC, in relation to the target event. Then, they start to focus on this new, positive belief. The BLS begins.

Phase 6 - Body Scan.
Phase 7 - Closure.

Body Scan

Sit in a relaxed position, two feet on ground, or lie down on back with legs a little apart. Let arms flop, palms up. Raise knees if uncomfortable.

Focus on breath - In through nose, out through mouth

Think of target event - Relay like images from a movie.

Become aware of body

Continue with BLS until calm, if needed

Distressing Memories of my own to work on

- Lying in bed, realising one day i will die and nothing will exist, total darkness
  I am unsafe, I will die, finality   Rating (10)

- The plane back from Australia
  I am unsafe, i will die   (9)

- Sleepless in Australia, calling Mum, (8)
  Dad won't stay with me until I sleep
  I am not safe, I am not capable, I am brok[en]
              I am mentally ill.

- Doctor assaulting me
  I am dirty, broken, defeated   (5)

- Taking citalopram, pressure, adverse reaction
  Something is wrong with me   (5)

- Dad trying to punch me   (4)
  I am unsafe, i am ugly and indese[rvable]

-

Group Therapy Course

Susie Hewitt — A tasker in working with and facilitating groups

~~Aims~~ Fatigued
1.30, 1hr, 3.30 - 15 mins
↓
Resistance

Aims

- evaluate your own experience of being in a group

- critically analyse various methods of running a group

- develop your own approach to leading a counselling group

Book - Developing Group Imago
Berne 1963

Imago - pichre we have in our minds

Provisional group Imago
Adapted group Imago

(* Looking at the one poc)

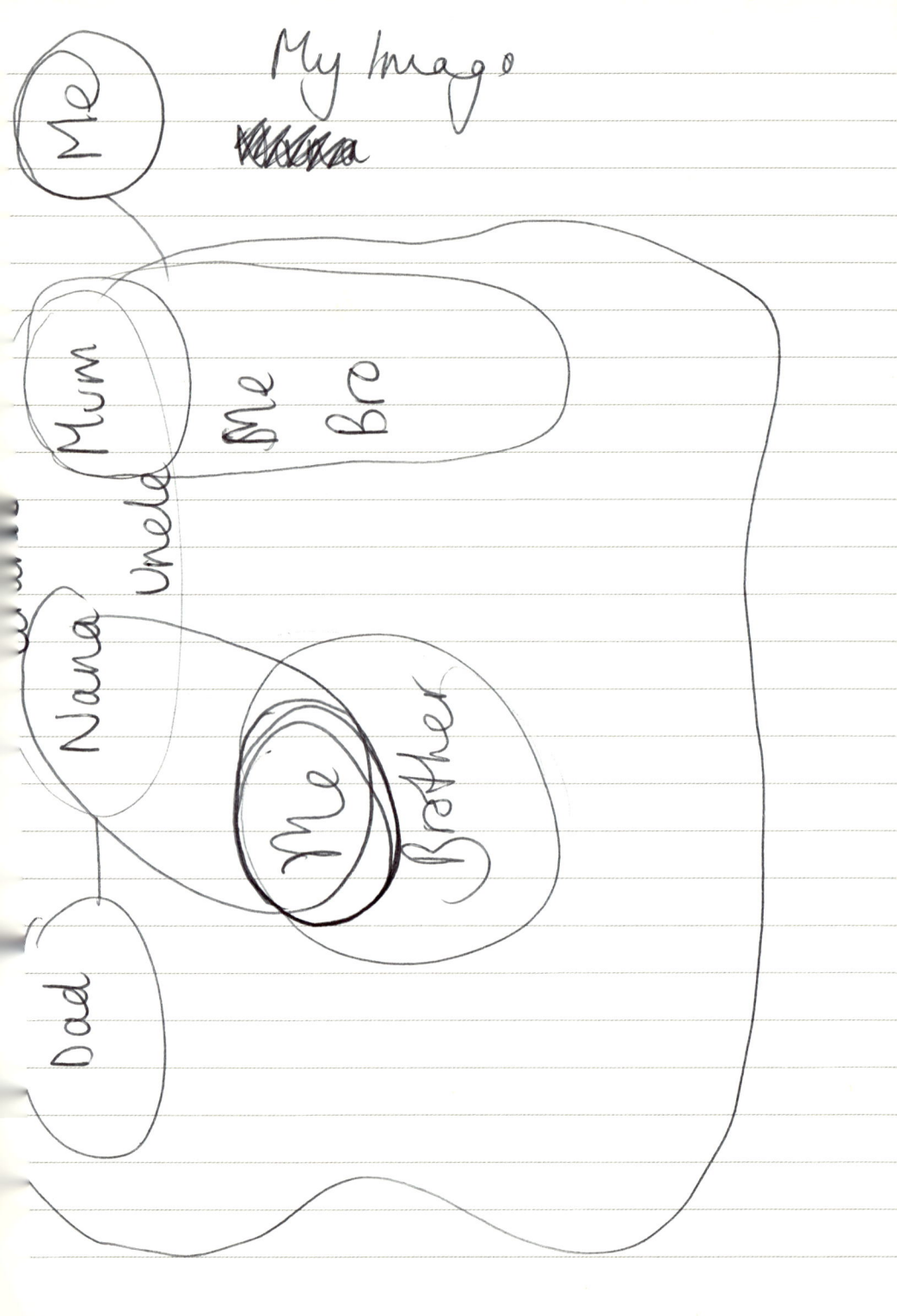

1st order structural Model

(P) Parental
thoughts/feelings/behaviour
Borrowed from them

(A) Related to here + now

(C) Replayed from childhood

Heterogeneous - randomised, non
(diversity)   controlled group

Homogenous - a commonality in
                  presentation

"Cushion work"
 - putting them on a cushion
   and speaking to them

What's showing up in client work
Do they have similar issues

"I am human, nothing human
    is alien to me."

How does group therapy help clients?
- Installation of Hope
- Imparting Information
- Universality — relief of meeting others
- Altruism — group member gifts others
- The corrective recapitulation of the original family group
- Development of socialising techniques
- Imitative behaviour
- Interpersonal Learning
- Group Cohesiveness
- Catharsis
- Existential Factors

Need to understand the unconscious original group family in order to recapituation.

---

ango(?) Interview Gabbole
    { Harry } Aan Seagul
    { Streaming live }
    { Pay per view }

My own Reflections (on operating group)

"don't be seen"
Resistance to the group/forced independence
A desire to find a "safe" person to form a sub group.
Not belonging in the group - feeling I don't have a place in the group
Reluctance to reveal anything

(Dad, (Tim + Grandad / Nana), Mum)
(Brother / Me)

hyperintune to "unsafe" people

Concerns
"On the verge of psychosis"

Stages of group development
by Tuckman, 1965

- ↓ Forming
- ↓ Storming
- ↓ Norming — openess, new standards
- Performing
- Adjourning — grief/attachment
  self evaluation

~~Patrishka~~ Clarkson (?) TA Groups
Patrishka "TA Psychotherapy Intergrated Approach"

Synthesising your own approach to Group Leaderships

Working with the individual
Working with the group as a whole

"What's going on in this group here already, and what's your part in it?"

What was lacking:
* Demonstrations of closing interactions
* Demonstrations of managing 'storming'/Transference

Co-Facilitative
Best - People who are in secure
Non-competitive
Aware of sibling transference

The courage to be me

by Dr Nina Burrows

Everyone is responsible for speaking.

This is a **FLAME TREE NOTEBOOK**
Published and © copyright 2014 Flame Tree Publishing

FTNB 53 • 978-1-78361-197-3

Cover image based on
Bal du Moulin Rouge poster
© Blauel/Gnamm – Artothek

Flame Tree Publishing Limited
Crabtree Hall, Crabtree Lane, London SW6 6TY, United Kingdom
www.flametreepublishing.com

All rights reserved. Printed in China